A Loose Rendering

Time, Memory, and Other Considerations

A Loose Rendering

Time, Memory, and Other Considerations

by

T. P. Bird

Golden Antelope Press
715 E. McPherson
Kirksville, Missouri 63501
2022

Copyright ©2022 by T. P Bird.

Cover by Rusty Nelson.

All rights reserved. No portion of this publication may be duplicated in any way without the express written consent of the publisher, except in the form of brief excerpts or quotations for review purposes.

ISBN: 978-1-952232-73-2

Library of Congress Control Number: 2022947401

Published by:
Golden Antelope Press
715 E. McPherson
Kirksville, Missouri 63501

Available at:
Golden Antelope Press
715 E. McPherson
Kirksville, Missouri, 63501
Phone: (660) 665-0273
http://www.goldenantelope.com
Email: ndelmoni@gmail.com

Contents

Dedication	v
Part One: Time & Memory	1
If You Knew the Yearnings of Aging Men	3
Of Time, Memory, and Other Distractions	4
A Man Takes a Walk in November Woods	6
In the Thinness of the Autumn Air	8
Remembering the "Village Tavern"	10
Red's Barber Shop	12
You Were One of Them	14
A January Night at the Orchard View Motel	16
Cafe Life with the Old Prof	18
A Little Bit of Vasana* Perhaps	20
Rereading the Dharma Bums Fifty Years Later	22
My Father's Memories of Black Creek Road	27
Visit to My Father's Hometown	29
A Night at the Theater	31
Conception # 1	33
Washington Park	35
Part Two: Poets, Presidents, and Me	39
In the Beginning	40
The Fabulous Fifties	42
The Sixties Begin	44
California Dreaming at the End of the Sixties	46

Somewhere Over the Rhine 48
Getting Away From Olive Drab 49
The Slippery Slope 50
Fighting Off the Darkness 52
Time Out of Mind 53
Deliverance 54
The In-Between Years 55
Into the New Millennium 57
And the Beat Goes On 58

Part Three: Other Considerations   **59**

Somewhat Observing the Perseids 60
An Instant Coffee Poem 62
Riff 63
Conception #2 64
The Voyage of the Rational Self 66
Getting by on Epigrams in
    a Non-Metaphorical World 69
A Postmodern Interlude 70
Monologue of a Man Trapped in an Old Journal 71
A Fanciful Chronicle on the Rewriting of Ancient History 74
While on the Bank of the River Styx— 76
The Refugee 79
That's a Good Question! 81
White Stones 82
Notes on a Search for Symbols and Metaphors 84
Of Tributaries, Rivers and Seas 88
Thinking About God's Waiting Room While Buying an
    Overpriced Latte at Starbucks 89
Contemplation in an Old Graveyard 91
Warning to Myself 92
Just Beyond 93
Sights and Sounds 94
A Fortunate Man 95

Acknowledgments   **97**

Dedication:

In memory of my father and mother
Paul T. Bird and Rita Saxe Bird

Part One:
Time & Memory

A Loose Rendering

If You Knew the Yearnings of Aging Men

If you knew the yearnings
of aging men—you would
know that their stories are
what really matter—and in

the telling, someone truly
listens, truly remembers—
even now, as well as in the
aftermath of this existing

world. For such are the
gleanings of a field not yet
left fallow to produce sorry
weeds and vicious briars.

If you knew the yearnings
of aging men—you would
hold them in your heart, and
know your stories are soon

to follow.

Of Time, Memory, and Other Distractions

Poets walk in circles—coming
back to well hidden, captured
thoughts—inspecting a mental
trap-line like trappers after pelts.
These thoughts perform for
an audience of one before being
exposed to the external world.
Thus, my walk takes me to
another snare.

‡

Standing in a group of men,
talking—a quick flash crosses
my inner sight, interrupting the
flow of my thought and
the conversation—if just for a
moment. It's a view of myself
as an aging man—no longer
relevant, afraid of descending.

It's also happened while I stood
before a mirror, shaving.
I saw my face grow out of focus
as steam washed across the glass.
Wiping at the reflection, a
stranger looked back out of eyes
like ice. The years are both a
friend and an impediment.

I can't go after old images
disappearing around a corner;
I might get terribly lost. Yet,
there is a great temptation to
explore. Only a lack of strength
will hold me here.

A Loose Rendering

I may laugh at the follies of youth—
yet, I grow impatient about the
impending conclusion of my life.
I see young bodies move with
ease—no pain in their rising
or falling. Often, I would like to
burst forth with bravado and
daring—to both conquer and
beguile the world at large.
Yet, the desire passes quickly,

amused at being noticed, a
mischievous smile at play in
the corners of its mouth. It will
probably return just for the
attention it receives. "Turn
away, turn away, go home,"
say I to my soul. It would be
folly to stay and wander; folly
to entertain distractions on
my way to other themes.

A Man Takes a Walk in November Woods and Asserts His Place in the World

> *[The blind man] looked up
> and said, "I see people; they
> look like trees walking around."*
> —Mark 8:24

Late November in the woods,
the hillsides—like me—have
suddenly gone gray with age.
It would seem, just yesterday
we looked young—running
crazy and wild across the
spines of the earth.

Single trees rise naked before
the world. Many appear old—
bare limbs like wisps of graying
hair, unable to cover their
baldness. Wooden bodies display
warts, whorls, twisted arthritic
limbs, and broken bones; all
entirely revealed— no longer
dressed in summer garb.

Are they embarrassed—unable
to hide secrets even from the
casual observer? I'm not here
to search out secrets, for I hope
to respect their privacy, using only
an unheralded, hidden glance to
notice their vulnerable condition.

Crows seem to scoff at elderly flaws
from the highest branches, their

A Loose Rendering

language unwelcoming as I step
through dry leaves that rattle and
crackle under and around my feet.
Despite the crows' taunts and insults,
I make no attempt at discretion or bunk.
And so, I shout out . . .

*Listen. I am an old man among
old trees on a very old planet,
and no smart-alecky young crow
is going to get the best of us.
So, put that in your boisterous
beak and choke on it—you
crazy, feathered fiends!*

I know those crows won't listen;
at least I got that off my chest.

In the Thinness of the Autumn Air

In the thinness of the autumn air—
no longer smothered in the denseness of
summer's humidity—we kids pulled on
sweaters or light coats and plunged
into fallen leaves of red and gold;
all nature's colors made stronger,
brighter—like the autumn sky with its
unabated blue.

        We raked and piled—
only to burst them apart with mighty,
unfettered cries of childhood joy, the
acrid smell of dried leaves in our nose
and captured in the material of our
clothes, and the hair on our heads;
parents always knew the chronicle of
our childhood day. Later, adults

would also rake and pile, yet would
not plunge, but burn our played-out
leaves in a ritual performed in the
days between winter coming and
summer past. Pungent smoke filled
the thinness of the autumn air, the
neighborhood scented with the raw
fragrance of this dynamic season.

Yet, now in fearful & disenchanted
times, bitter smoke has been sent
away. Dry leaves are stored in big
plastic bags—dispatched to lonely,
unknown places. I seldom see kids
kicking and jumping in autumn
leaves of red and gold; they too
seem exiled—perhaps to cyberspace

game-rooms and organized play—
seldom experiencing sights, sounds,
and smells that abound in the
thinness of autumn air.

Remembering the "Village Tavern"

It's an era when tavern life is common in America—some years before the vast seeding of ubiquitous fast-food chains—especially in small river towns like this one with its locally owned bar and grill. Our family has driven here on a number of Saturday afternoons, brought by my restless, hard working dad, and willingly housebound mom. Sometimes, after receiving our drinks, we wait on an order of burgers and fries.

For the most part the tavern's long room is filled with eerie dark shadows, where the ghosts of patrons might sulk over perceived past insults. Tiny wall lamps with smoke-discolored shades hang from dark paneled walls over wooden booths—giving just enough light to reveal table tops. The smell of stale beer and cigarettes hangs in the air, along with the vague scent of my mother's perfume. Half-lit parental faces lean over the table like conspirators plotting a coup d'etat, talking in cryptic grownup language that I don't try to follow. My younger brother sits back in the booth next to my mother with his own five-year-old thoughts. I sit next to my father, nursing an orange soda—knowing I won't get more—and observe the soft glow coming from the bar area at the end of the far reaches of the tavern. From there, I hear faint chatter and the fits of laughter of men and women sitting on tall stools—the sight and sound of which is mostly a mystery to my fertile eight-year-old imagination. I munch from a small bag of chips whose salt inflames the cold-sore on my bottom lip. However, I'm not willing to stop eating this tasty treat.

Here I sit contented until nature calls for an emptying of my bladder. I know I'm too old to be taken to the restroom, and so I must traverse alone the dark territory between here and there, beyond lurking shadows, beyond the seated strangers at the bar, beyond the door of a room marked Men—an entry into another world altogether. My father notices my squirming, and tells me

A Loose Rendering

to go and pee. I protest weakly; he raises his voice just a pinch, and I know I must brave the journey.

It seems a walk of a thousand miles—shadows and bodies going by in the corner of my eye. Feeling neither my feet on the floor, nor the brass knob in my sweaty hand as I turn it, I enter a small room with sour smells and a sticky floor, and head for the urinal in a kind of haze. As I relieve myself of bladder tension and the remains of orange soda, I look about. Above my head, small color photographs of naked women hang on the wall like angels without wings—hovering in the sour air with garish, bright red lips and rosy nipples. I find myself in a different kind of trance—one that is unfamiliar, alien to my eight-year-old mind and imagination. I linger, but finally leave, the shadows and the presence of strangers no longer a menace on my way back to my parent's booth.

The fries and burgers have arrived, and we begin to eat. All the while I wonder if my parents can magically read my mind. For, I revel in the idea of returning to that little room without actually knowing why.

Red's Barber Shop

One Saturday morning of the month during the 1950's, my Irish mother, like an army drill instructor, sent my brother and me marching off to Red's Barber Shop; her orders: get it cut short, just short of a close shave. Red was *the* barber in our part of town, and Saturday—the busiest day of the week at Red's—his shop was always crowded with men waiting to get neat for the week. Ironically, Red was the one in the room with the least amount of hair.

Red's shop was a boy's portal into a man's world—sitting among older males who talked *to* no one in particular, but *at* everyone who would listen. Red, a taciturn fellow (not a phrase I would have used at the time) said very little in reply when talk was aimed at *him*. Red spoke mostly in the language of his trade: scissors—*clip, clip, clip*, shaver—*buzz, buzz, buzz*, then the *scrape, scrape, scrape* of his straight razor cutting through foam on the back of one's neck like a plow pushing through fresh snow.

Those who didn't talk, read magazines—picked casually from a cluttered table or an empty chair, mostly without much forethought. For a young boy, perusing the pages of *True, Field and Stream, The Saturday Evening Post,* and *Life Magazine* was another entryway into the mysterious goings-on of the grownup world. Mind you, you found no smut at Red's—except for an occasional glimpse of innocent native flesh in *National Geographic*.

Due to some cosmic mishap that happens in many barber shops across America, time slowed down dramatically in Red's shop. Young boys often get stranded in an eddy of the fourth dimension—going round and round, but going nowhere. My juvenile brain made it appear as if Red was operating in ultra-slow motion—with decades passing while customers sat in his chair, clippings swirling above shrouded bodies like dust motes circling in sunlight before falling to shoulders and floor ever so laggardly, Red and customer not moving a muscle all the while.

How could the month displayed on the wall calendar stay the same while we waited for our turn!? Patience is not a young boy's best virtue.

‡

    Suddenly, time speeds up to its normal course. Finally, the hour comes when we get to sit in Red's chair, my brother first, then me. It's a moment of reckoning—the moment our drill instructor mother has ordained. I climb into the antique barber chair and Red pumps it up. He doesn't ask how I want my hair, he has a direct line to my mother's mind. Now, under the white shroud, I gaze upon Red's display of bottles and jars filled with strange potions for head and hair—similar to a mad scientist's laboratory in a scary movie. The paraphernalia of his labor lays about, waiting a performance in the master's skillful hands. Combs—plunged into a white-cross marked vessel full of a mint green watery substance—have been fractured in two by some mysterious bending of light. Then a small click . . . the shaver's buzzes are bees circling around my head, waiting to come in for the kill! The clip, clip of scissors—a giant insect with fierce mandibles approaching from behind! Shaving cream is slathered cool behind my ears and neck. I feel the tender touch of Red's sharp razor against my skin; I'm about to be clawed by a beast of prey! A towel is used to staunch my wounds, *Lilac Vegetal* slapped on to cool and repair my body. A paper collar and the shroud come off in a swirl of tiny hairs; a small broom-like brush sweeps over my clothes. I rise from the chair, pay the man, and my brother and I retreat thankfully out the door and back into our familiar boy's world—neat for our mother and the coming week.

You Were One of Them

—for Lynne

In my life many people have
passed through far too quickly.
After days, weeks, and six months
of working with you in Ft. Ord's
old hospital, you went home
while I was away at my own.
I still harbor loss; our good-byes
never existed—just the missing
words that were never said.

I was a young man, maybe
more of an over-ripe boy—
an innocent—shy, and perhaps
considerate without even
meaning to be. You, a few years
older, were a warm smile in a
small frame, a light voice from
the upper Midwest. I knew of

your hometown's name—yet,
none of its life and stories.
But it was okay; my recognition
forged a link between us. Maybe
a small thing, yet I will always
remember the small things.
They flash by now like passing
railcars at a lonely crossing;
like oncoming autos on a busy
highway, your face in each and
every window.

You seemed wiser, more knowing—
having seen pain, suffering, even

A Loose Rendering

death—attending to the bodies of
eternally young soldiers—a cruel
time for a lovely, dark haired girl
in olive drab and lieutenant's bars.

The nurses' station at the
beginning of our hospital shifts
was like a lifeboat—as the
names of patients were lifted
from the churning waters around us.

Often, when we shared shifts,
I felt your smile and calmness
from afar—a gift from across a
barrier of rank and duty. Your
eyes, like a message among other
messages, stayed upon me longer
than needed—keeping me from
falling overboard into my own
sea of inadequacy. I'm sorry
I never thanked you for that.

Many people in my life have
passed through far too quickly.
You were one of them.

A January Night at the Orchard View Motel

My long drive south through the
State of Pennsylvania (literally with
a long delay over the Susquehanna)
ended at the no frills Orchard View Motel.

I settled in, but restless after many
miles on the road. A bright winter
moon with a halo in a buttermilk
sky threw light upon old snow with

a thick coat of ice. I was called out
into the cold, crystallized air like a
man under a sorcerer's magic spell.
I couldn't resist its compelling draw.

Strolling up the orchard road—the
ice under my feet crunched loud in
the windless, cold air. Then, naked
apple trees glistened before me in

the heavy moonlight, ice enveloping
their bony, awkward branches like
casts on helpless, brittle limbs—
many down upon the frozen ground.

I stood, silent in the raw evenfall, and
listened for the sound of desperate
whispering among the icebound trees.
Nothing, except the faint yapping of

a small dog farther up between the
burdened trees. Soon, it appeared at
the edge of the orchard—only to
retreat at seeing a stranger, its little

A Loose Rendering

legs churning above the frozen snow
like the spinning wheels of a snow-
bound car. Could someone else be
sharing my ice-charmed orchard on

this frigid night? In the solitary stillness
of this place, I suddenly felt time and
myself held in the grip of ice; the trees,
the earth, the entire world frozen in place.
All things asleep until the angels wake us up.

Cafe Life with the Old Prof

for Dr. David L. Thompson (1940-2020)

>For four years I met with
>this retired professor of
>biblical languages on
>Tuesdays for lunch and
>conversation at a local cafe—
>two aging men among
>academics, students, and
>others roosting for an hour
>or so under low-watt lights,
>the hum of voices and the
>occasional scrape of a
>wooden chair across a bare
>cement floor in need of
>new paint.
>
>I asked my endless questions—
>while eating a chicken salad
>sandwich on a kaiser roll and
>sipping aromatic coffee—
>my mind anxious to stimulate his
>toward a didactic romp
>through his expansive learning.
>(Once the romp led us on a hunt
>through the school's library for
>content on the ancient Semetic city
>of Mari, the old Prof full of pep.)
>
>Without condescension at however
>odd my questions might be, he'd
>diagram his answers on a napkin
>or write out a series of words as
>the burger on his plate grew
>cold and forgotten before him.

A Loose Rendering

Struggling with Parkinson's, his
legs silently aching under our table—
once provoked, he'd teach with a
renewed vigor, adding self-deprecating
humor when at a loss for a good
answer to my constant probing;
true humility filled the spaces
between his brain cells and the
chambers of his heart, making
his words not only interesting,
but also full of wisdom.

My old friend, the Prof, is
gone now—succumbing to age
and that terrible disease.
The cafe where we ate is
now silent of our conversation,
our laughter, our joy together.
I'm hoping the Prof remembers
to reserve a table for two in
some heavenly cafe, where we
will resume our Q & A—both
of us knowing the answers in
advance.

A Little Bit of Vasana* Perhaps

Occasionally, like others, I get
sudden mental impressions
of the past . . .

I'm maybe nine or ten,
and lying in a sick bed.
I've been there most of
the day reading comic
books or sleeping.
It feels to be around half-
past five in the afternoon
on a pleasant autumn day.
The window of my bedroom
is slightly open;
the air outside is just getting
seasonably crisp.
I can hear the neighborhood
kids outside playing without me—
voices full of childhood fun
and excitement. I feel strange;
for the first time in my young
life, I'm experiencing loneliness.
However, soon their sound will
fade as they are called in for
supper by their mothers.
I'm already feeling better.

☦

At twenty-one, I turn from
the mirror in my army barracks
deep in the heart of Bavaria.
A quick flash of youthful well-
being washes over me—all manner

of things seem clear, life is my
oyster, the possibilities are endless.
Is it a transfer of energy from one
source to another, or is it just
vernal ignorance?

Call it what you will, the past
never leaves, nor do you leave it.

---

* "Vāsanā (Sanskrit) is a behavioral tendency or karmic imprint from one's past, which influences the present behavior of a person. It is a technical term in Indian philosophy, particularly Yoga, as well as Buddhist philosophy." —*Wikipedia*

Rereading the Dharma Bums
Fifty Years Later

"Days tumbled on days, I was in my overalls, didn't comb my hair, didn't shave much, consorted only with dogs and cats, I was living the happy life of childhood again."
—Jack Kerouac

Fifty years ago . . .
Just days "in country,"
I was sitting in an
army ambulance—
a jeep shrouded in
drab brown blankets
to keep out the winter
cold of Bavaria—
motor running six
hours straight, trying
to pump heat into our
mechanical cocoon
while M60 tanks practiced
firing their guns
at an imaginary foe.

My companion—
a taciturn soul—
was no doubt
unsure of my recent
posting to his
medical platoon:
was I a narc?
(lots of hashish was
being smoked by
young American G I's),
or just a guy dumped

A Loose Rendering

into central Europe to
play soldier for a year?

I'm glad I brought
Kerouac's book
with me—though I
don't remember
buying it, or even
finding it. But there
it was in my ungloved
hands, sentences
punctuated by the
boom of big guns
in the frigid air.

Like Kerouac's
tumbled days,
the hours tumbled
by as Ray Smith,
Japhy Ryder and
their recusant pals
romped through
Zen-filled pages
with a super-extended
bohemian protest
of the mundane
American life.

Barely twenty-one,
more a boy than a man,
I gladly traveled along to
poet, Alvah Goldbook's
(Ginsberg) reading (*Howl*)
at the Gallery 6.
Later I drank wine
while talking into the
night by lantern-light

with Ray's fellow
"birds of a feather,"
while carousing with crazy,
over-sexed girls; we
hooted and hollered haiku
at each other like
brokers before Wall
Street's "Big Board."

I climbed the High
Sierras with Ryder and
Smith (Gary Snyder
and Kerouac),
sleeping in cold, thin
air and sharing Ray's
fear of heights and
falling off a mountain,
recovering when he did.

I rode with Ray in a
gondola on the Midnight
Ghost from LA to
San Francisco;
hitchhiked with him
cross-country on the
virtuous mid-century
highways of America;
and ate cheap meals in
greasy spoons.
All intoxicating.

All the while the DATS
("dirty ass tankers")
hardly fazed me during my
fanciful literary fling.
I take it my fellow jeep
sitter never noticed

A Loose Rendering

I was missing in action.
At the end of day we
headed back to a large,
mostly unheated tent
and cold C rations.

‡

Fifty years later . . .
wine and green tea
still flowed. As I read
Ray and Japhy were
still doing their
"beat generation"
thing—Ray still
ducking yard dicks
and generally
sloughing off 50's
conformity; Japhy
still climbing mountains
and waiting for the
world to change in order
to accord with his
nonconformist beliefs,
and wildly flung
sophist declarations.

Perspective is everything.
No longer caught up
in the spell of
The Dharma Bums,
Kerouac's work
now seemed to me a silly
incantation—meant to
carry both writer and
reader far away from
any unkept obligations
of an ordinary life.

His magic was meant
for those who long for
perpetual adolescence.

Reading Kerouac
fifty years later,
I found myself sad for
my lost youth.
It's not Kerouac's fault;
somehow I left it behind
with that young soldier
in a cold jeep, the fuel
of fascination in the
gas tank long running
on empty.

My Father's Memories of Black Creek Road

My father's past had all but disappeared
from this lonely country road in the
Appalachians of northern Pennsylvania.

It was late August, we had driven here
in his new time-machine—a red Buick
Skylark—on a daylong excursion through

his early years in two rural counties—
full of tree covered hills, deep vales, stony
creeks, derelict pastures, small deserted

stores in little rundown hamlets—where die-
hard hill people hung on with a tenacious
love of place. My grandfather Clayton

tenant farmed on Black Creek Road for
three years in the late 1920's. All that
remained decades later were lilac bushes

on a steep knoll beside the road; house,
barn and outbuildings—long gone. With
no place to park along the narrow and

curvy route, we didn't climb the knoll and
explore where his large family had lived
in those times. Perhaps my father could still

see its outline against trees and sky, and
that of the barn across the road; if so, he
kept this to himself. Down Black Creek, a

mile or so, were the remains of a one room
schoolhouse—now a stone foundation filled
with rotting wood, leaves, and rusting pieces

of metal. A memory of wintergreen covering
the ground near the school could not be
verified with any present sight. The sound

of children playing, until a bell called them
in, was so long ago, it had finally faded
away, escaping through the hills and valleys

until not even my father's memory could
capture it. My father's older brother John,
a person with a rebellious and wild nature,

once assaulted the young male school teacher
for supposedly 'picking on' his younger
brothers. My father then recalled one

winter evening when he and my Uncle
Gene were late coming home from school
after playing in a frozen Black Creek.

My grandfather met them in the barnyard,
rather annoyed that they'd missed their evening
chores. It was not a happy homecoming

for two boys who once lived on Black Creek Road.

Visit to My Father's Hometown

Driving the back roads and haunts
of his early years, my father and I
entered the town of his birth via

the 'back way'—the main road
before US 220 was built with steam
shovels and the force of men's will.

We passed the house where his life-
long friend, George K., lived as a boy
in knee pants—an abandoned and

crumbling shell with faded yellow
paint and a sagging front porch—from
which his mother yelled at the three

brothers who always got her son into
childhood trouble. Though our windows
were open, we drove by too fast to hear

the ghostly echo of her angry words,
nor the brothers' crazy laughter as they
ran down the hilly road towards home.

Following the way, old houses appeared
where neighbors once lived—their names
now mostly forgotten, occupied now by

strangers with different sets of memories.
My father recalled an old apple tree,
now fallen down behind a strong stone

wall that once fenced in grazing sheep;
no animal now stood in the tall grass of
the empty pasture. In his memory, those

apples were sweeter than Eden's own
fruit. Saint Basil's, where a young boy
rang the church bell three times a day,

was a mandatory stop—almost sacred
to an old man's sentiment, the sting
of a nun's rap of knuckles still felt.

Standing on the cemetery hill behind
the church, his young self ran wild again
through the town like a passing storm.

A Night at the Theater

Attending a Christmas concert with my wife at a local high school, I watched young teen performers on stage—singing, dancing, playing their parts with great spirit—all causing my thoughts to travel back to my own senior year as a "stage manager" for our annual high school talent revue. The title suggests something far more glamorous than the actual role I played—lugging props back and forth, horsing a piano on wheels across the stage, removing leftover debris: 'grunt' work with the mental strain of knowing what act came next and being prepared.

My thoughts took me back to a special moment of that night. I noticed a girl with me in the wings—a bit younger than me—a member of a previous dance number. We both watched the current act on stage, I anticipating my next move, she standing next to me—close enough I could feel the heat from her exercised body. She mentioned that their act was good. I don't remember replying. She lingered through a couple more routines. I admit to stealing glances at her, wondering why she hung around, more than half hoping she'd continue to do so. Another act appeared on the stage. The girl again stood close by. It was nice having her stand there next to me. Was it the atmosphere of the 'theater,' the congeniality of working together to put on a show? Was it a kind of 'spiritual' thing, sharing a moment in our young lives that might not have happened otherwise? Or was it just plain old hormones at work in an adolescent boy's body? Most likely all of these.

From out of the proverbial blue, I felt her arm on my shoulder as she lightly leaned on me. Why would this young "dancer" with nice legs want to lean on me—a skinny stage hand with glasses and untamed hair? How did I react? I played it cool and remained aloof—pretending not to be affected by her touch. It all too soon passed: she went away and I finished the night up—the proverbial lonely stage hand who never got the praise or the glory for a job well done. And, as you might guess, I never got the girl either.

Yet, now in my imagination . . . *I find myself standing in the dark wing of my old high school auditorium. I'm watching a single spot of light on the dark, empty stage beyond. I'm just watching, waiting for a warm hand or arm to rest on my shoulder. At its coming I turn around, saying "thanks" to a person I don't recognize, yet know who it is by her touch. She no longer is a pretty fifteen-year-old girl, but a woman beginning to notice how time slips away. She smiles warmly, and asks, "Thanks for what?" I say, "For the memory." She says, "Oh . . . I was wondering if you would remember." "Of course I remember . . . I just don't know why." Continuing to smile, she looks out to the stage, now filled with cheerful sound and bright lights, but nothing else. "It's a good act." she says. I reply sincerely, "Yes, it certainly is."*

Conception #1

The past is just recognizable here at the corner of Sturdivant and Saylor Roads—two dirt lanes atop a rural upstate hill—still farmed in present time. Here are the remains of an old homestead: a three-sided foundation among a small grove of old growth locust; a great stone slab on the near side to Saylor, which may indicate the house's front entrance. An old lilac bush testifies to a likely home for people who once lived and worked this piece of ground. Were they possibly the Sturdivants or the Saylors? One can conjecture as to what lives transpired in this quiet place. . . .

The late spring evenings are pleasant, the day's work hard since early morning. But now, the ending of the day will bring rest and a sense of satisfaction and wellbeing—despite the hardships of farming the land and living off its bounty.

The wife and mother of the home takes a few moments to sit on the front stoop, and watch her children play in the dooryard. Cries of laughter and excitement do not distract the flow of her thoughts. In fact, this is the music that plays accompaniment to her heart's song.

She is waiting for her man to come home from the nearby fields, where he has been plowing behind a horse since the noontime meal. Here is their little corner of the larger world. The air that fills it is theirs to breath; the fragrance of lilac and supper cooking on the fire lifts the senses beyond the smell of unpleasant farm odors. She knows this little house will shelter them adequately against the darkness and the unknown of a country night. How little she asks of life— content to be a part of God's creation, having a place and purpose in the grand scheme of things. On the next morn, she knows they will rise and prepare for the wagon ride to the little church in which they will worship with their far-flung neighbors; theirs is a life of gratitude and subtle reward. Yes, she knows uncertainty, sorrow, weariness, sickness and death will visit their lives; each will stand on their front slab, knocking to enter. However, tonight as the evening breeze cools the flesh and brings forth the lilac's scent, she reflects on more blessings than one family can possibly handle.

These are not the memories of the people who lived here all those decades ago. Their memories faded away somewhere along time's journey forward. I sometimes wonder what it would be like to see other people's memories play out in my mind as if they were mine—not through words in a book or conversation, but viewed through some kind of hidden metaphysical mystery; perhaps like a 'visual' *collective consciousness*. I guess we are truly alone in our visual memories, yet, never far from the fellowship of humanity as we share what we remember . . . or even what we remember for others.

Washington Park

After Frank O'Hara's "I do this, I do that" Poetry

1.
Banners in the June sun exhort
me: *Celebrate Washington Park*—
a design of green, ringed in red with
brick row houses under a light blue sky.

So, I exalt the big canopy beeches
with amputated arms and wings like
bats, oaks—solid and heavy with hair
like Medusa, gnarled old maples,

knuckles full of arthritis. I exalt the
locusts with trunks like barber poles,
and the 'tree of heaven' with its ancient
warts and angel wings at the end of its

branches, flying among the star-like
leaves of a nearby sweet gum tree.

2.
I *Celebrate Washington Park* and
applaud Albany's lunch hour ladies
who trade office shoes for sneakers
to stride among mid-day joggers.

Silently, I cheer on the old guys, half
bent over, chatting airily with each
other, while they admire the young
women—quiet and serious in their

runner's ritual, coursing among men
with ties and ID badges. I cheer on a

stiff–armed blond with a capacious
behind under a flowered dress.

Should I extol the wannabe beauty
as she appraises the boys with their
big bounding dogs? A cigarette hangs
from her painted mouth like an arrow

in a bulls eye. Sure, why not?! I
commend the Albany cops keeping a
relaxed watch over playground kids,
and praise the little black girl gliding

off with dad on training wheels down
a beaten path—heading somewhere
into tomorrow. Here's praying all goes
well on your journey of life. Be safe.

3.
Here at midday in Washington Park,
space and time stop stretching; every
thing holds back for an hour or two.
Even the statue of Robert Burns, with

his floppy hat in hand and fat finger
marking a book, comes alive—a
bemused smile on his blackened-
bronze face as he watches the traffic

flow beyond neatly laid rose beds.
At noon space and time stop stretching
so a quiet man can sit against the trunk
of a towering tree, its leaves shading his

thoughts from the heat of the sun, while
a bare-chested fellow with a pony tail
greedily soaks in its rays through a haze
of cigarette smoke. Everything waits as

A Loose Rendering

>two women sit at a picnic table peering
>through photos like CIA analysts, while,
>nearby, a haggard gray haired Joe in a
>dirty baseball cap reads a newspaper
>
>and picks his nose. Everything waits
>until I greet an oncoming giant with a
>*"how are ya?"* and he looks up with a
>sudden smile and proclaims,
>
>*Considering this beautiful day—I*
>*would say, definitely, I'm doing good!*
>
>— *Albany, NY 2006*

Part Two:
Poets, Presidents, & Me

A Semi-Epigrammatic History, Both Public & Personal

*"I feel like saying it's the poet's job
to remember. . . . Remembering
is the art of the cave dweller."*
— Gerald Stern

*"Acting together with character,
circumstance accounts for the chaos
of history–its twists and turns."*
—Jacques Barzun in
—From Dawn to Decadence

In the Beginning

Conceived, born and nurtured
in W.H. Auden's *Age of Anxiety*,
my life was early kissed by fear
and embraced by the shadow of
nuclear madness—for Harry Truman
had used FDR's BOMBS, destroying
two Japanese cities and killing over
200,000 civilians—yet, keeping my
soldier father alive for the sake of my being,
which entered the space-time continuum
thirty days after Thomas Dewey didn't win
the presidency in '48—despite the headline
in a now defunct New York newspaper.

Robert Lowell had written, *Lord Weary's
Castle*, gaining a Pulitzer and certain fame.

Dylan Thomas was romancing his way
through numerous drunken readings with
his Welsh diction—finally, *Go[ing] not Gently
into that Good Night.* In November, '53
Thomas collapsed into an alcoholic coma
at New York's *White Horse Tavern*, later dying
in a nearby hospital. A talent gone far too soon.

William C. Williams had begun his literary walks
through *Paterson*, trying to understand the
quickly changing world as only he would;
reading *Paterson* years later, I was only confused.

As I sucked on my bottle in my mother's
clothes basket, I never imagined the
"Beats" were early exercising their hipster
desires. Neil Cassidy, Jack Kerouac,

A Loose Rendering

Allen Ginsberg, and William Burroughs
remained mostly unknown while I,
a toddler, tumbled down some hard and
heartless concrete steps—gaining early
a primal glimpse of life most poets and
prophets would understand. In the abyss lay
Langston Hughes' *Montage of a Dream Deferred*,
together with "crazy" Ezra Pound, imprisoned
in his *Pisan Cantos*.*

---

* It is said Pound wrote this collection while held in a cage in Italy by the military in 1945. He had been arrested as a traitor for broadcasting on the radio propaganda for Mussolini's facist government during World War II. Later Pound was sentenced to a hospital for the insane in the U.S. He was released after twelve years through the efforts of many fellow poets, including W. C. Williams.

The Fabulous Fifties

"Give-em-Hell" Harry then chased
that old soldier Douglas MacArthur
out of Korea and into a hasty "fade away"*
because the General esteemed his military
genius way too much—wanting to take his
wary troops into China.

    Later, Dwight Eisenhower, war hero,
beat out Adlai Stevenson in '52 to usher
in the world of Ginsberg, Lawrence
Ferlinghetti, Diane Di Prima, Kenneth Koch
and Robert Creeley—all hoping to shape
a lemming nation into a poetic
                       "counter-cultural ethos."
However, Ike gave little credence to *Howl*,
cool jazz, poet Gregory Corso's illicit cravings,
or Frank O'Hara's poetic 'New York doings.'

    All the while . . .
my childhood adventures were simple:
eating Gram's warm homemade bread & sugar;
buying penny candy and soda from Haner's
corner store; exploring bug filled giant peonies
in my aunt's backyard; madcap Karen
aping me in the first grade lunchroom
as I ate my mushy white-bread sandwich.
These, among others, made my decade wild.

No photos of Walt Whitman, T.S. Eliot, Emily
Dickinson or Robert Frost hung in my father's house.
H.W. Longfellow, Joyce Kilmer and Ogden Nash
made cursory appearances in my elementary school—
without, may I note, studious interest or critical revue.
Lowell came back in '59 with his own *Life Studies*,

A Loose Rendering

making 'confession' more than a religious practice,
while winning another Pulitzer Prize, as I watched
westerns on TV and listened to the Yankees finish third.

* General MacAuther would later say, "Old soldiers never die, they just fade away."

The Sixties Begin

In '61 a young, handsome John F. Kennedy
invited an elderly Robert Frost, who—
blinded by the January sun—recited a poem
with faultless memory at Kennedy's inauguration.
Two years later he took his *Gift Outright*
with him into the ages. Then, as I commenced
to conceive of poetry in the curve of schoolgirls'
splendid calves, the famous "battle of the
anthologies" broke out on the academic front.
No fatalities were reported.

Then came the 'dream-fixed' poems of
John Berryman and the strong and desolate
verse of Sylvia Plath*—both, unfortunately,
doggedly dragging their addictions and
neuroses with them, as I daydreamed of
girls' pretty faces and other things.

Meanwhile . . .
in the upper Mid-West, James Wright landed
on a sturdy branch and sang a different song
with his collection, *The Branch Will Not Break*.

Bill Stafford, pacifist and beloved mentor to many,
hauled a dead pregnant deer off the road while
                    Traveling Through the Dark.
Probably his most anthologized poem.

W.D. Snodgrass painfully threaded *The Heart's
Needle*, trying to put his life back into one piece
after a nasty divorce.

A Loose Rendering

Living out west in the wilderness—Gary Snyder
read and wrote poems by the stars and firelight.
 He would later put out a winner with *Turtle Island.*

Eldritch Knight, carried out of Korea nearly dead,
entered a long and fateful prison stay
and devoted himself to the writing of poems.
He would later say, "poetry brought me back to life."

⁂

For a thousand days Kennedy presided over
the nation from "Camelot," until a dark and
mysterious Lee Harvey Oswald reportedly
murdered the president while he rode in a
motorcade through people-lined Dallas streets.
I heard the news over our school's PA speaker,
while struggling to learn the language of
Julius Caesar.

For days a shocked and grieving nation
kept vigil before their black and white televisions
as the thousand days of "Camelot" came to a close.
Lyndon Baines Johnson was sworn into office in the
presidential jet. This began the turmoil of the later 60's.

Epigrams are not cool at recounting such a time in history.

---

 * Sylvia Plath, best known for *Ariel* and her novel, *The Bell Jar*, committed suicide in 1962. She had been suffering from major depression, and possibly long-term bi-polar disease.

California Dreaming
at the End of the Sixties

As the days of the decade journeyed on,
my thoughts were not on poetry—but on
a girl two desks up and to the right.
Yet, slowly, I awakened to Bob Dylan's
poetry-like lyrics and folk music's lonely
tales, while LA's boozy Charles Bukowski
recalled in a poem "a dog barking senselessly
somewhere." The hound, no doubt, foreknew
LBJ's damn war in Southeast Asia*—replayed
for us daily on the evening news—Cronkite**
                          barely hiding his liberal burn.

And out came the poets of protest: Robert
Lowell wrote an open letter to Mr. Johnson.
Robert Bly, W. S. Merwin, Adrienne Rich
and others labored at poetic dissent and
proclaimed a solidarity as I got carted off to
basic at Ft. Dix, New Jersey in February of '69.

No photos of Walt Whitman, Eliot, Frost,
or Ezra Pound hung on our barrack's wall.
Bly, Ginsberg and Denise Levertov never made
a showing on the parade ground as I stepped
off to Ft. Sam Houston to learn the fine art of
                          a combat medic.

That's okay—Dylan was the only poet I knew.
Bukowski would come later—even after I found
Leonard Cohen's *Selected Poems* hanging out on
Monterey's bird-pooped wharf. God bless *half*

A Loose Rendering

crazy Suzanne down near the river. And God
bless the anthologies of Hall, Hollander and
Strand, along with Penguin's *Modern Poets*—
plowed like rich soil over chili in a downtown
diner while I waited for my hospital shift to
begin at Ft. Ord, CA.

                    I don't know if Mr. Nixon
ever read these versifiers. The Commander-
in-Chief never knew I copied Wallace Steven's
verses on a 3x5 and taped it to my locker door.

Yet, it was as Jack Gilbert's poem has said:

                            "Question
The bravery. Say it's not courage. Call it a passion.
Would say courage isn't that. Not at its best....
It is the normal excellence of long accomplishment."

   * The U.S. had a military presence in Vietnam from 1964 until 1973; 58,220 American combat deaths and over a million Vietnamese deaths resulted.

   ** Walter Cronkite was a long-time anchor for CBS Evening News. Cronkite, a staunch liberal, kept his feelings and opinions to himself over the years he reported the news on television. His signoff became an American institution: "And that's the way it is on . . . ."

Somewhere Over the Rhine

Escaping the existential threat of a steamy jungle,
I jetted off to the Czech border to drive around
eleven tons of steel with a red cross on its sides.*

Ah, but the poets came with me—traveling ahead
in the pages of poetry books, stacked—not so
neatly—on the post library's dusty shelves.
How I treasured their company as we trundled
back to my cave behind the lockers with writers
like Updike, Gardner and Malamud joining us
for quiet, book-filled reveries.
                        Oh, how I wanted to join them
at building a more circumscribed world. And so,
while others played chess while stroking their
mustaches, I wrote lousy poems out of an
                                    experiential void.
The Soviets apparently didn't care to complain;
                        they never came over.

---

* I was part of American NATO forces for a year, assigned to a medical platoon in an armor battalion, stationed in Schweinfurt, West Germany. The vehicle mentioned was an armored personnel carrier (APC).

A Loose Rendering

Getting Away From Olive Drab

Traveling to Paris on leave with my quirky friend Paul,
I drafted weighty verses about sipping French coffee
on Place Saint-Michel, while watching people erupt
from the Metro like lava from a fiery peak. One could
almost hear the ghosts of Valery, Baudelaire, and Apollinaire
moan low as they stole a look at my scribbling and went
away laughing, strolling together along the banks of the Seine.

Later . . .
Lovely Barcelona would blossom like a flower after seedy
Marseille required an abstraction—and so, we hurriedly
took the rails south along the coast. I recall pushing
my thoughts against the railcar's black window. The night
had crowded in, swallowing all but my weary reflection.
Then, the Spanish chatter of our fellow pilgrims—common
people with chickens and tied bundles—grew as we crossed
the border like refugees in the depths of the Iberian night.
How Paul and I admired the beauty of the Catalonian women
in the late glow of the Barcelona station lights!

The Slippery Slope

Returning home in February '71,
how I aspired to get into print—
gathering enough rejection slips
to paper a small room, while, sadly,
Berryman jumped off a bridge, and
Ann Sexton closed the door on her
troubled life.*

Meanwhile, John Ashbery looked into
a *Convex Mirror* and won himself a Pulitzer.

After waving as if anybody cared, Dick
Nixon flew off in disgrace from the
White House lawn, leaving Gerald Ford
to come and go in a flash as Jimmy Carter
moved up from Georgia, once confessing
lust in his heart to an interviewer from
Playboy magazine.
Jimmy was more open and honest than
most men across America—including me!

Haunted anew by Auden's anxiety, I laid
low in my cave with a wonderful wife and
soon two kids, scrawling poems of angst—
angry about the imagined darkness just
outside my door:

> *So as the golden days pass into*
> *the blackness we crave, we leave*
> *bits of ourselves on bar-tops and*
> *half empty glasses of good intentions*
> *we never finished or even tried.*

*It comes so hard–the waiting for
the last chance to redeem our lives.*

Where all this came from—I was never sure.

* John Berryman, the poet of *Dream Songs*, killed himself in '73. Berryman had a long history of alcoholism. Ann Sexton, a "confessional" poet, committed suicide in November of '74. She suffered from bi-polar disease. Sexton won the Pulitzer Prize for poetry in 1967 for her book *Live or Die*.

Fighting Off the Darkness

While I struggled to remain calm and viable,
the poets of the 70's passed before my eyes
"in a swelling chorus," thanks to an anthology
by Edward Field—*A Geography of Poets*—and
joined me from the four corners of the land.

Within its pages I was introduced to names
I'd never heard of or read—including many
women poets: Tess Gallagher, Kathleen Norris,
Lucille Clifton, Louise Gluck, Marge Piercy,
Marilyn Hacker and others. They nightly joined
my reading under a dusty bedside lamp—
opening up new visions for me from the
feminine side of humanity.

Yet, these fine surveyors of verse could not
keep my mind from slipping into the darkness
that now engulfed my cave—nearly wasting
all that I was or ever hoped to be. As Carter
spoke of a perceived "spiritual malaise" overtaking
a weary nation, I wrote a few plaintive lines from
the hospital mental ward:

> *The bones of my body–*
> *even to my skull, are*
> *hollow as empty cartons.* *

---

* In 1979 and '80 I suffered from clinical depression. I joined the list of poets and writers who have suffered with some form of mental illness. (www.therichest.com/most-influential/10-of-historys-great-poets-who-suffered-from-depression/)

Time Out of Mind

The poets failed to join me in my bewildered state.
Neither Hart Crane, Plath, nor Sexton hunkered with
me in a smoke-burdened lounge filled with haggard
spirits, while we waited on pills or a dose of electric
shock. Yet, I must confess, I didn't invite them to come.

Hiding from my psyche's hollow pain, I cowered with
a cheap paperback below the dark clouds that hung just
inches above my bed. Carter didn't send a get-well card.

Deliverance

Like the earth, the heart turns in an orbit.
From solstice to solstice, it travels around
the things we fear unto the One who loves—
while, from equinox to equinox, it journeys
from empty longing to what a heart truly needs.

So, I traveled through the night on Dylan's
Slow Train Coming and wakened to Reagan's
"Morning in America." Yet, the light didn't come
from the White House, nor from poetry shelves in
cluttered bookshops, but out of the darkness slowly
left behind—revealing a path ahead to "greener
pastures, stiller waters."

I returned to my cave in submission and received
a hidden strength. Seeking the heavens, I gained
earth's blessings. Embracing the "Ground of Being,"*
I found my soul renewed.

---

* One of theologian Paul Tillich's names for God.

The In-Between Years

The Reagan and Bush (one) years passed quietly
for me, while sacred prose and contemplation
filled my cave with a consummate holy fire.
Few poets came while I journaled my way through
the tangle of the middle years—the versifiers' absence
hardly noticed, nor my exile from their company
ever fully understood.

Then Bush (one) wisely cut short a desert war,
but forgot to button his political lips, and the
economy tanked—allowing Bill Clinton to overcome
a number of dubious affairs, engendering his wife
as a partner of political convenience.

I read much prose and some poetry by Donald Hall,
spending hours at Eagle Pond Farm, wrapped both
in his past and an ever-present present. However,
it was the quiet poems of his wife, Jane Kenyon,
floating and drifting in a *Boat of Quiet Hours*—
that awakened me to the possibility of my poetical return.
Attending to her half-hidden and mindful reflections
on New England life, love and home—and unaware
that her understanding of nature in *The Pond at Dusk*
had already come to completion—I read with sadness
in the back pages of *Constance* that she had died
of Leukemia in '95. It was as she wrote:

> "But sometimes what
> looks like disaster is
> disaster: the day comes
> at last, and the men
> struggle with the casket,
> just clearing the pews."

As Clinton, an effective leader, unfortunately stayed true
to his wandering nature, Robert Hass—all West Coast
consciousness—stirred in me dissimilar *Human Wishes*;
I too believed I could smell laurel, fennel and thickets
of broom while caught up in a spell of casual conversation
and quiet observation.

Into the New Millennium

Despite such inspiration, my muse and pen stayed silent;
old and half finished poems remained dormant in folders
and spiral notebooks as the world went by with barely a nod—
passing just outside my cave. Yet, the poets of the new
millennium came to fill my leisure hours with their witness
                of the world.

At the new millennium, Bush (two), who came to power
boosted by a hanging chad, soon went to war against hate-filled
zealots, while Ground Zero in NY lay in ruins—a grim reminder
of a sad and grievous world. And what did the poets & prophets
have to say? Much. But with a nation too angry with grief to
listen—the wisdom of our better instincts was drowned
in the awful howl for another battle with the modern ruler of
Babylon. And on it went as we tried to hide our eyes from
the reality of broken bodies and the sting of nettled nerves.

"It is good that war is hell," a famous general had said
many years before, "or else we would grow to like it."

Then, "mission accomplished" gave way to "hope and change."
As Bush (two) went back to Texas in '09, waving goodbye
to the Obamas standing on the steps of some official building,
many poets entered my cave to spend the hours.
Even Mark Van Doren, Mary Oliver and Gerald Stern came
in death and old age to center me in a time of transition.

And the Beat Goes On

And change is always here as I sit before my cave in a time of
Trump and Biden, constant turmoil and political struggle.
Poets will come and go from my over-stuffed shelves
                like minstrels on a tour.
And as they do, I will listen, learn, and remember—and yes,
I'll write *my* poems of witness and speculation—
my means of seeing, recognizing, and naming
                this crazy, considered world.

The ideas I offer may be dispersed like seeds—apprehended by
an incidental few. Nonetheless, I ask, does my obscurity and
randomness really matter? I think it best to put away my played-
out aspirations and wait patiently for an answer. It may come
in a 3 AM dream, or as I walk in the winter woods. Either way,
I must think to make some detailed notes when it does come.

Part Three:
Other Considerations

Somewhat Observing the Perseids

One Friday night in mid-August,
I drove the family up on Saylor
Road to observe the annual
Perseid meteor shower. The

best night—two days earlier,
was cloudy and wet, the weather
refusing to open its curtains on
the celestial show. Parking the

car at the edge of the dirt road,
we climbed out into the country
darkness and the small sounds of
insects in the fields around us.

Facing northeast, we looked for
a heavenly display. Being
beyond its prime viewing time,
we had to be alert for the few

fiery streaks that crossed
through Earth's aura. There we
stood, leaning against the car,
heads craned back, staring into

the black sky to see if the
comet Swift-Tuttle was still
letting out passengers on its
journey through the Milky Way,

which ran overhead like a busy
freeway around a city at night.
Betwixt sporadic strikes, light
conversation filled the empty

spaces in the watched sky—
accented with oohs, aahs &

shrieks when a passenger left
the speeding ball of ice and rock.

After a time the position of our
heads in relation to our shoulders
caused quite a kink in the neck.
Later, I lay in the backyard on

a chaise lounge, hoping for a
later performance. All I got
was our cat's company and a
wet, cold blanket of dew.

The rewards of a true stargazer
can be an exciting experience.
But, I'm afraid, not always.

An Instant Coffee Poem

After reading
an anthology of
"Coffee Poems,"
I made a cup of instant,
and sat down
in the middle of
an imagined coffee
plantation, and myself—
a single bean—
trying to write a poem
about being planted,
picked, shipped,
roasted, packed,
stored, sold, ground,
run through hot water,
poured, and inhaled
before being swallowed by
a yawning black hole
in some strange cosmos
of a coffee shop—
whose pull of gravity,
sucked me into a vast
space beyond, where
I mixed with other
tired travelers.

This poem can only
end somewhere in the
vast recesses of this
city's bowels. The
reader, if not happy
with my taste, may do
with it what they will.

Riff

If it's a true poem,
it gets laid down
on paper like a jazz
player circling and
swirling around a
melody line—
finally coming back
to finish the thought
after a time away.

And all the while
the reader gets lost
in the cycle of words—
all like musical notes
bouncing around in
Saturday night's
heavy air—looking for
form . . . until they
finally rest somewhere
in the imagination.

Conception #2

A nondescript woman is soaking in an old clawfoot bathtub. It's in a non-modernized bathroom of an old farmhouse. She is reading poetry aloud, wanting to hear the sound of her voice caressing the words, the verses, the stanzas. It is very important for her to hear them—being that she is unsure of the veracity of her internal ear. She is alone in the house; no other voices or distractions will disturb her recitation. The window is open; it is the height of summer. The air outside is moving gently—lifting the edge of the curtains. The breeze moves on, carrying with it the voice of the woman reading words aloud, the verses, the stanzas of a poem.

The air moves on its route across a lawn that needs mowing, across a tired dirt road, and down through an aged apple orchard with its gnarled trees half bent over like very elderly people. Unbeknownst to the woman reading in the bathtub, these old trees can hear her voice—have been secretly listening from this orchard to the sound of voices for a long, long time. The trees have very old limbs—weary with a tree's equivalent of human arthritis. The sound of the woman's poem helps the trees to imagine, once again, a full harvest of fruit hanging heavy from strong limbs in the coming autumn season. Yet, even if the sound of the poem is comforting, they know that the rings of a tree's life are hidden beneath their brittle bark; any thoughts of abundant fruit is just a dream.

Yet, the old trees hope that she or he, or they, will wander down across the old dirt road and linger among them. It has seemed a long time since people living in the house have carried on a conversation under their limbs. It could be casual talk, just sharing anecdotes. Even mulling over the folly of politics or the newer philosophies would be okay; these trees have never been ignorant of humans' tendency to blow things out of proportion. What they really long for are the brace of human emotions to hold up their aching limbs and tired branches. They remember the sound of lovers' murmurs as they slyly shifted from tree to tree, wading through shin high grass, hoping for a stolen kiss, perhaps more. And later, children's squeals and laughter as they played under the white glow of spring blossoms.

This poem is the first time they hear the voice of the woman in the bathtub. This ancient orchard does not really know who these new people are; and the life of these old trees is unknown to these people. Perhaps they will finally notice the trees in the old orchard, and visit; the old orchard would love to hear the sound of more poetry.

The Voyage of the Rational Self

I
In the beginning, when he set
out on the open sea—that
ancient symbol of chaos,
confusion, anxiety and fear—
unshackled emotions and
thoughts ruled his ship like
a tyrant, piloting his vessel
like a drunken captain—
often toward the imagined
safety of shore, not reckoning
that rocks awaited in
anticipation of his ruin.

He would have to push
this unsound master aside,
and consult the charts, get
his bearings, and steer a
course despite a heavy sea.
More than half the crew
deserted ship, casting
lifeboats upon the waters,
unsure of the fitness of one
who stops to think his way
through the roiling waves:
they could not believe that
wisdom and reason, like a
sextant, could navigate
them safely by way of a
starry, waterless ocean
above.

What remained of the company
were unsure sailors, whose

A Loose Rendering

maiden voyage had begun
under a directed intellect's
authority. Uncharted
waters lay ahead, safe
harbors—a tenuous hope
when the seas became a
plight. Yet, the new
captain would examine
the sky and keep his logs.
He would stand his watch,
look for evidence of good passage,
and store in his logbook
what proved to be true.

II
His old ship is still sailing,
at least for a time. His
crew has been mostly
loyal, some still wary of
the master's cryptic ways.
He must watch the seas for
pirates—those who would
plunder his treasures: truth,
goodness and beauty, setting
his mind adrift—those who
would take away his sextant,
and leave him to the mercy of
fickle winds.

In numerous lonely nights,
his thoughts have kept him
company, his feelings
listening to their talk. Yes,
some have argued the
direction and speed of their
course. He takes these doubters
to the bridge deck,
and shows them the stars.

He asks them plainly:
just what, by chance, my
friends, might you have
in mind?

Getting by on Epigrams in a Non-Metaphorical World

Perhaps, as you read this piece you may think it *a title in search of a poem*. Maybe, but I think it too early to tell. It may simply turn out to be a poem in search of a better title. I've seen a number of those in the "best of" anthologies.

Anyway, I like this title—at least for now. Perhaps we should give it a chance to explain itself . . . like maybe in a podcast . . . if we can find the right kind of host who asks the right kind of questions; perhaps a doctor of letters? No . . . too pretentious; the *avant garde* won't listen to such stuff.

Perhaps this title wants us to think about bad poetry? Something like the following . . .

> *Let me share another sign*
> *of human weakness: after*
> *picnicking under the shade*
> *of a maple tree, I am tired—*
> *body and soul—just from*
> *eating hot dogs, salads and*
> *baked beans, while listening*
> *to the talk of others and me*
> *talking without much purpose*
> *other than filling the obligation*
> *of sociability.*

The above could possibly improve with a good title. But, it must understand—the title of this poem is already taken, along with its epigram.

A Postmodern Interlude

> *"[The] currents of postmodernism
> mirror the morning-after hangover—
> we are trying to sort out the night
> before so that we can get a handle
> on the day at hand."*
> — James Emery White,
> in "Serious Times"

According to some thinkers . . .

it's been a long, drawn out hour
since discontented hearts found
a good word to use in the dark;
artful talk no longer comes easy.

Fingers speak only doubt with
an accent of brooding angst.
The deceit of passion is gone;
the demands of intimacy are
beginning, and no invention is
definite enough.

So now we must mimic words
like deranged, paranoid parrots,
and fabricate a lie from what
remains of a language that has
no meaning.

Left to decipher the world's cunning
from an ever growing list of illusions
and narratives empty of veracity,
we creep from our beds—
hoping to walk upright again. . . .

So say some thinkers.

A Loose Rendering

Monologue of a Man Trapped in an Old Journal Since Thursday, January 14, 1993

1993 was the Year of the Rooster

David Letterman announces his show is moving from NBC to CBS

Polish ferry boat capsizes in storm, 50 die

"Anna Christie" opens at Criterion Theater NYC for 54 performances, starring Natasha Richardson and Liam Neeson

The number one song in the US on this day was "I Will Always Love You" by Whitney Houston.

Toronto Blue Jays beat Philadelphia Phillies (4 – 2) to win the World Series.

    1.
Many men search for lost emotions
through hectic days and sleepless nights.
Young men dream of success, trying to

slice it off like slabs of meat or cheese—
consuming it without gratification,
while older men lunge at shadows,

grasping the air like pickers of fruit,
pulling at the limbs of the sky
for any sign of life, or anything that

resembles the life they once had.
To relieve stress, the voices of these
anxious men (All men are anxious;

some hide it better than others.)
often launch into conversations like
sailboats in a brisk wind—the waters

not calm enough to enjoy the ride.

For the sea of one-up-man-ship rises
and falls upon the bow of fragile boats

full of words; waves of indifference,
even condescension, can run smaller
craft hopelessly aground on reefs.

Yes, the reefs are there; be careful!

2.
I'm afraid these words may be an
example of non-direction; best not
follow them as instruction adequate

to reach your goal. Possibly,
they are just the ramblings of a man
suffering "the slings and arrows of

outrageous fortune." If you so choose—
ignore them as you would a bore at a party.
Remember, these are only an attempt,

though feeble, to communicate something
to someone (even one's self). If you
cannot relate to them, do not be concerned

or feel clumsy. Ignorance should not be
considered a compromise; after all,
the world is compromised enough to

fit any situation. There are many
comfortable ways to ease the tension
from these awkward moments.

Perhaps you could remember the first time
you fell in love. But don't linger too long;
you will only fall back into endlessly

scratching at the sky, searching in places
that can't be found. However, in the end
you must suit yourself. These words may

belong to any man who finds himself
trapped in an old journal. However,
the rest is up to you.

A Fanciful Chronicle on the Rewriting of Ancient History

*In his Poetics, Aristotle maintained the
superiority of poetry over history because
poetry speaks of what ought or must
be true, rather than merely what is true.*
—found on Wikipedia

I.
Early humans, or our prototype—
the first historians without PhD's or
published papers, left their observations
on the cold walls of caves: animals
running from spears and arrows—
an ancient reminder of the postmodern
proverb: victors write the histories,
not to mention getting all the spoils.

II.
Out of the once 'Fertile Crescent' came
the cuneiforms—secretly chipped by
early 'deconstructionists' to alter stories
put out by the writers of local history.
Even Egypt's hieroglyphics may be
seriously muddled—raiders of tombs
mixing up painted symbols, confusing us
about what really happened. The madness
of revisionism came early, buried in the
sand until ideologically needed.

III.
The geeks among the Greeks threw
out the gods and all their egotistical
rantings—Herodotus and Thucydides

leading the way to the 'historical method,'
yelling in chorus: "It's cause & effect;
don't you get it? People are history!"

IV.
And so, if people are history, then people
make history, later write history, while
afterwards, other people rewrite history.
Keeping an account seems a mug's game.

As if anyone cares, I'm with Ari on this one.

While on the Bank of the River Styx—Just After a Supper of Beans & Franks with Nietzsche, Duchamp, Cocteau, Cage, and Foucault

> *"Last sound, the world going out without a breath:*
> *Too proud to cry, too frail to check the tears, and*
> *Caught between two nights, blindness and death."*
>
> —Dylan Thomas, from his unfinished poem, "Elegy"

Earlier in the evening,
five voices filled a small,
dim cottage by the River Styx*—

a cockeyed conversation
between modern vanguards—
an artist, a poet, a composer

and two philosophers—
let loose temporarily from
the confines of an endlessly

tongue-tied eternity.
These men helped open
up the 20th Century to

absurdity, nihilism, and
eventual despair. My
curiosity about culture,

and this poem, had
brought them here for
one night—to hear from

whence it all came.
We shared a meal together
of beans and franks,

bottles of cheap wine
and baskets of stale
bread, and exulted in

the imagined glow and
heat of a burning hearth.
Unfettered voices merged—

likened to wind
and rain in a furious
storm—while sudden

shouts flew up like
the sound of the agitated
beating of large wings.

I just listened in silence
to their pointless talk of
fragmentation and life

as chance. After the meal
and outside on my own,
while the others continued

in their *ad hoc* immunity
from death's silence, I
walked along the dark

river, noticing that I left no
tracks in the ever-present
snow. I thought upon

the night's conversation,

but remembered no
cohesion in their dialectic—

only a forced synthesis
of the irrational. Reality
seemed a distant star.

Walking along the River
Styx, the night was dark,
still, and deeply cold—

with a feeling of
emptiness at having been
"deliberately destroyed."

Yet, my breath—a chilled
fog before me—assured
me I was still alive

and writing at my desk.
My faith in antithesis
was affirmed: "If a thing

is true, the opposite is
not true; if a thing is right,
the opposite is wrong."

Otherwise, I have become
nothing.

---

* "In Greek mythology, Styx is [a goddess and] a river that forms the boundary between Earth (Gaia) and the Underworld." —*Wikipedia*

The Refugee

To live below the line of despair [life without meaning] is not to live in paradise, whether that of a fool or any other kind. It is in a real sense to have a foretaste of hell now. . . . [S]ensitive people have been left absolutely naked by the destruction.
— Francis A. Schaeffer

Other refugees from perceived folly may be traveling tonight under the cover of darkness; the border between madness and rationality isn't as secure as earlier reports would have us believe. Are there other figures darting between the blackened trees like wild animals lingering on the edge of extinction? Are there others running in the opposite direction, hoping to escape from reason? I jump in fear, thinking a shadow moves over me. How foolish to think I would be so easily seduced at this stage of escape.

The wind is up, moving bony limbs like oars in the dark sea of this absurd forest of strange times. I want to shout, laugh, scream, anything to break the tension. Then it strikes me: how alone I am in this frontier between states of mind and will. Regardless of other possible expatriates from a realm seemingly gone crazy, I feel alone except for the chilled breath I give out. I begin running toward the razor sharp wire of the border. Branches cut and slash at my face and hands. I feel no pain, only anger at knowing that many are against me because I chose to escape, anger at a possible loss of freedom, and at any attempt to prevent me from escaping.

I listen for words like gunfire over my head—and am ready to duck and dive, ready to find safety and solace in the soul-preserving truth of an absolute. Still, I find myself crawling through dead, rotting leaves, and the wicked roots of nihilism. They turn over and over in my suddenly confused mind—trying to ensnare me, keeping me from breaking free.

Just when I feel my strength to be at its end—border wire, taut and fierce, looms above my head—*Down! Down*, I silently scream, *Get under the damn wire! Crawl on your belly like a frightened snake!* I propel myself like a burrowing mole deeper into the earth. I pull forward, just inches more—the final push. Having entered refuge I am exhausted, but satisfied—even while counting the cost. Looking back across the border I can only hope madness will eventually die of its own doing, slaves returning home from self-destruction.

That's a Good Question!

"What's the difference between coexisting and cohabitation?" my wife once asked out of the blue while we traveled in the car.

Let's see if we can figure this out . . .

We can exist without cohabiting, yet we can only cohabitate if we exist.

Coexisting means getting along okay with those we exist with.

Among humans, to cohabitate usually means not only living with others, but also having sex with them.

Yet, my dictionary says to cohabit also means animals coexisting with animals of a different species—yet, they don't have sex with them.

On the whole, humans find it easier to cohabitate than to coexist; people seem to like taking the path of least resistance.

But the real difference between people and animals is that some people are willing to spend time writing poems about such questions—questions that are best left to the squirrels in the yard and my dog who chases them. Maybe between them they can work it out.

White Stones

Now it is many years beyond the fifteen the poet
Archibald MacLeish wrote from in 1933—as he
spoke to dead soldiers buried in rain soaked
Flanders fields. In his poem, *Lines for an Interment*,
he told them life had gone on without them—that
polite and refined people occasionally mentioned
them while they drank their afternoon tea and ate
their biscuits and cakes.

And now, the graves have grown in number
beyond that Belgian meadow . . .

> too many graves in
> even more meadows;
> too many names
> on white stones.
>
> Too many names,
> forever young,
> engraved in
> now mostly
> overlooked
> hometown
> monuments.
>
> Too many names
> in the shiny
> black wall in
> Washington DC—

all far from the scene of their hallowed honor.

Like wildflowers their bloom was beautiful
and all too short.

A Loose Rendering

And the white stones of every military graveyard
cry out in moonlight for justice, for retribution
against the mad men who imposed their

>dark ideologies,
>their arrogance,
>their will to power

onto the lives of the innocent, the disarmed,
those who wanted only to grow into old age,
and fall asleep listening to the rain fall gently
                              on the good, good earth.

Notes on a Search for Symbols and Metaphors in Southern California

1.
I was once told by a learned man
the stories of men are written or
told in symbols and metaphors—
for it is the nature of humanity
to think of the world in this way,
to make record of sudden quirks
and anomalies that play out their
strange existence in concrete time.

2.
Take for instance—the bench on
the other side of a glass wall in Balboa
Park on which I went to rest, but
found I was on the wrong side of
the glass.
> *It could be a*
> *symbol of isolation*
> *in a world of*
> *ubiquitous self-*
> *induced bubbles,*
> *or simply a*
> *trick played on*
> *a mind far from*
> *familiar places.*

3.
How about my daughter's bearded
dragon, who excited himself on my
laid-aside jeans—his beard going
black in the throes of his carnal
desire. Later, it was reported he

looked pleased with himself—
half smiling, lizard eyes half shut
(or open) after the final results of
his reptilian fantasy.
> *A metaphor, perhaps,*
> *of intimacy with the*
> *pervasive symbols*
> *of American-styled*
> *freedom that never*
> *meet our deepest*
> *needs. Or just a*
> *miniature Godzilla*
> *run amuck among*
> *my clothing.*

4.
Let me not forget how I sat on a
green crayon left on the back seat
of my daughter's car, wax silently
sealing shut the rear pocket of my
already abused jeans, only noticed
later when the day shifted to night.
> *How long did I*
> *walk about in the*
> *dazzling sun with*
> *this mark of instability,*
> *this emblem of my*
> *failure to be hip in*
> *a hipster's world?*
> *Most likely no one*
> *cares if I am or not.*

5.
My daughter shared with me a
vision of angels hovering over noisy
children in a nearby swimming pool,
and the peace it bore. In the telling

angels milled about *her*—the one
who sat on her terrace astonished—
her turmoil and the doubting world
fading away with each flutter
of a wing.

> *I would venture*
> *there are always*
> *answers to the*
> *questions we ask*
> *ourselves—even*
> *while drowning*
> *helplessly in the*
> *density of our pain.*
> *What else can it be?*

6.
I'm still searching for a metaphor
as I remember our trip to LA—
staying overnight in an *ad hoc*
boarding house—bare-bones, our
room empty of decoration, end
tables, lamps or carpet,
the bathroom down the hall with
slates on the shower floor that
drooped under the weight of my
wobbly, wet body. Feeling afloat
under the shower's spray,
I imagined myself a sailor on a
slick deck in a storm-tossed sea . . .

> *Perhaps I was*
> *traveling between*
> *places of meaning,*
> *and needed to adapt*
> *to the uncertainties*
> *of the age in which*
> *I live. Or it was the*

> *result of a limited*
> *budget.*

7.
Walking on the Venice Beach boardwalk, I jokingly thought of holding the sleeve end of my empty jacket out away from my body, as if I too, like so many around me, were holding the hand of a lover.

> *Oh, the losses we*
> *suffer as we move*
> *through the abstract*
> *motions of life—*
> *even in sunny*
> *California. Or I was*
> *feeling far from my*
> *wife in a city of much*
> *make-believe.*

8.
My learned friend knew it all too well. Our *lives* are the symbols and metaphors from which the world draws its amusement. Strange—that we would see ourselves as a straight-forward discourse that all can easily follow, while never acknowledging the aberrations and anomalies that tell us who or what we really are. Oh, we foolish humans!

Of Tributaries, Rivers and Seas

Every day—thoughts, beliefs, emotions, affections, and desires flow into the bed of our psycho-spiritiual rivers like tributaries—streaming mountain run-offs making their way into the steady current of life and living. Eventually, all our rivers merge into the deeper waters of Durkheim's so-called *collective consciousness*.

And so, when the heart bursts forth with positive human passions like love, joy, mercy, jolts of sudden happiness, a sense of well-being (*Shalom*)—tributaries run ample and rivers swell to good abundance. We then say, "The river looks healthy today," as we observe it from the shore of our conscious selves. When life, however, becomes troubled with rejection, frustration, disappointment, and anger—self control breaks down; unlovely passions like sudden violent storms, cause flood waters to rush into our rivers, overflowing the banks, possibly taking down what has been carefully built up.

At the risk of sounding pedantic—if one looks indifferently, without discernment or wisdom, the tributaries flowing into our psychic rivers may appear clean—seemingly free of heart's corruption. Without careful keeping, they may fill with the sad litter of pessimism, fear, the irrational—hatred, bigotry, and violence finding their way into moving waters, polluting our rivers, ruining the sea of Durkheim's *social forces*. Deeper within their waters—dangerous currents and obstructions from all quarters may await the unwary, soul-weakened swimmer. Remaining in such waters, we could forever lose the old memory of good and evil, right and wrong, and why it matters that we know the difference.

A Loose Rendering

Thinking About God's Waiting Room While Buying an Overpriced Latte at Starbucks

"The creation waits in eager expectation for the sons of God to be revealed . . . in hope that the creation itself will be liberated from its bondage to decay and brought into the glorious freedom of the children of God."
—Romans 8:19, 21

While waiting in the drive-thru lane, I look about:

It's early April—aglow with the white, red, and
pink buds & blossoms of spring, the wallpaper
God chose for his waiting room—at least for this

season of my life. That is to say, things change:
the smell of earth and the scent of man, the feel
of breeze or breath upon one's cheek, the taste of

words—like different coffees—spoken to others
(or one's self). What you hear from about (or from
within) are all reminders that one's never sure what

to think is true of (or in) this fugitive world. Here in
God's waiting room we all hope to hold off the last
of summer's shining rays upon our bodies, the descent

of autumn's final leaf, its sound as silent as a tomb,
or the final snow of a long hard winter. Too many try

to hold back the end of what they know of life, while

expecting nothing more. Yet, by faith, it's here that
creation and I await life anew in the promised age
beyond all this. Though creation's present beauty can

amaze and stir the soul, creation and I both know its
cold, certain direction toward death and decay—and
that is why, though clothed in spring's attire, we hope

for more; even knowing little of its endless abundance.

A Loose Rendering

Contemplation in an Old Graveyard

What better place to think about the meaning of this earthly life than in an old graveyard—where the bones of the dead lie buried in the earth, and under a sea of grass, ground-ivy and sweet violet.

Sitting on a crude stone bench under tall, aged trees, it's easy to look upon gravestones, and recognize there's a beginning and an end to everything in this weary old world. Engraved names attended with the simple phrase, *gone but not forgotten,* ring hollow after hundreds of forgotten years—even as moss, lichen, time and weather have hidden or worn away the many names of those we are to remember. And so, a stranger will wander in this quiet place, perhaps intrigued by a sense of history and the mystery of life's passing—either quickly or slowly—unto death. Many strangers will come away and try to forget all they learned in this silent neighborhood of the dead. Yet, those of certain faith will come away—assured their names will be remembered by the one, of whom, it really matters.

—The Pisgah Cemetery, Woodford County, KY

Warning to Myself

> *"The heart is deceitful above*
> *all things and beyond all cure.*
> *Who can understand it?"*
> —Jeremiah 17: 9

In the strange context of
my times, I find myself
running backwards up a
road I just came down—
feeling the need to protest
all possible protests,
rage all possible rages, and
deny all possible denials.

As I battle the man in the
mirror, I know I must not
let him see the fear in my eyes—
yet, I find I can't look away
from his. He watches my
every move.

What appears to be true,
it takes a dreadful moment
to understand: that to renounce
either mystery or revelation
is to live without hope in the
terrible reality of the world's
inescapable imperfection.

I'm not sure I'm ready to live
with that or die in the longing.

Just Beyond

> *"If we confess our sins, he is faithful*
> *and just and will forgive our sins and*
> *purify us from all unrighteousness."*
> —1 John 1: 9

From where I sit in human solitude,
I see just beyond the tangled, leafless,
winter shrubs, a patch of flowing creek
on its way to a distant place just beyond
the veil of my limited faithfulness.

Yet, now in my mind this selfsame water
remains for me—hope sparkling in the sun
like diamonds, or perhaps like a far
city, seen from a black sky at night.

As my attention is drawn to water and light,
I sense Him washing and anointing my feet—
freeing my soul from a terrible, undefinable
distance between us.

Suddenly, I understand there's no reason to
live in regret. For nothing exists but mercy
just beyond the self-made limits of God's
                                        memory.

Sights and Sounds

> *"For since the creation of the world God's invisible qualities—his eternal power and divine nature—have been clearly seen, being understood from what has been made, so that men are without excuse."*
> —Romans 1: 20

Plants and trees bend to the light
in secret. Space folds and curves
in the embrace of gravity, while
time pays attention to speed. All
nature heeds the laws of physics,
their patterns set before us without
possible change or protest.

Yet, humanity resists the bending,
the folding—once fallen into a pattern
different from the intended course of
divine will. All creation looks on with
fearful understanding, shaking its
sorrowful head, hiding itself from
humanity's foolishness and rage.

Yet, at present, I walk with a given faith
through fields, forests, and city parks
and look and listen as nature reveals God's
love to me in its native dress and language—
the sights and sounds of hope in our redemption.

A Fortunate Man

It would seem all my years have
come the distance to walking this
creek day by day with my hound.
Ginger runs with youthful strength
from smell to smell—occasionally
looking back to see if I still keep
my eye on her; and I do. Yet ...

at this moment, slightly stunned, I
watch—not her, but the setting sun
strike the top of tall sycamores with
limbs like the whiskers of a catfish,
turning their brown leaves of late
autumn into gold.

A gentle creek, the setting sun, tall
trees, a loving dog, and ... it all speaks
to me. Living to know such good things,
I recognize, despite all this world's woes,
I am a most fortunate man.

Acknowledgments

- "In the Thinness of Autumn Air." *Trouvaille Review*
- "My Father's Memories of Black Creek Road." *Tiny Seed Literary Journal* (in a different form)
- "Visit to My Father's Hometown; Washington Park." From my chapbook, *Scenes and Speculations*
- "Poets, Presidents and Me. *Footnote/Alternating Current Press* (in a different form)
- "While on the Banks of the River Styx"; "Of Tributaries, Rivers and Seas." *The New English Review.*
- "Thinking About God's Waiting Room." *Ekstasis*